APPLE GARDENING

How just three small spindle trees will ignite your next gardening adventure

Mason Vollmer

ISBN 13: 978-0-9967168-3-3

TABLE OF CONTENTS

What About That Big Old Apple Tree / A Little Background / Apples 101

TABLE OF CONTENTS

About That Big Old Apple Tree…

Recently gave a presentation to professional arborists representing municipalities, commercial tree care companies, and educational organizations, all promoting the benefits that trees provide. Yet, only one out of over 200, attendees was familiar with the Spindle technique that solved the challenges that big old apple trees pose long ago.

It's not just professional arborists who have yet to learn how the Spindle works, but Cooperative Extension educators, Master Gardeners, and many more. The Spindle technique remains largely in the realm of large scale commercial producers, yet it has profound potential for small scale gardeners interested in multi-functional, sustainable landscape systems.

In the world of Arboriculture — bigger trees are seen as better — in terms of providing the plethora of environmental services we love about urban trees, including; shade, energy savings, carbon sequestration, beauty, and much more. But with Apples it's different. Why? Because of three biological factors characteristic to the Apple. 1-The nature of Pome fruits 2- The transformation of woody structure and apical dominance 3- The influence of rootstocks in form and fruiting. All three of these factors combine with the cultural practice of the spindle technique such that — smaller is more efficient. This is counterintuitive yet true, because of the special biology of the apple. **Here's a 3-minute video on that** https://www.youtube.com/watch?v=ARsmH1jH_BI

The Spindle
"A Big Little Tree"

You're about to learn the most efficient and exciting technique — What I call the "Little Big Tree"

Spindle Trees = *Apple Gardening* instead of Big Old Orchard Trees

In the same space that one large tree requires, you could have twelve varieties coming into bearing in just a few years and ripening over a four- to six-month period every year. That's efficient for both space and time! Your mini-orchard can include rare heirloom varieties, new releases, easy-to-grow disease-resistant types, red-fleshed apples, specialty cider and culinary varieties, and more. Having a collection that's small and manageable is a gardener's delight. It's so scalable: if you find a variety that you love and want to grow more of, you can easily add more trees, or remove trees that are working. With small trees, everything is easier. Yields vary, of course, but a six-year-old spindle tree can yield between 0.5 to 1.5 bushels per tree (or 20 to 60 pounds), depending on variety, location, and conditions. This also means every Apple Garden can be a curated collection — preserving endangered varieties.

A Little Background

I love growing tasty veggies, fragrant flowers, health-enhancing herbs, friable soil, rich dark compost, and more—*but most of all I love growing gardeners, arborists and educators.*

I'm a horticultural educator who has been using bio-intensive gardening methods for more than 40 years in school, community, and backyard gardens in various regions of the United States, supporting nonprofit organizations that serve folks of all ages, abilities, and backgrounds. A garden that "grows people" has all sorts of fertile soil for growth: including educational, therapeutic, prevocational, environmental and social justice opportunities. Still, every garden has its own human and site-specific challenges.

Yet if I could suggest one horticultural technique to you, it would be the apple spindle method. I daresay the spindle method works better than the espalier method (which I've used in the past). Spindle is easier, quicker, and more accessible for you, your family or students, and your community to start growing in ways you have yet to explore.

Ah the right tool . . .

We've all had that experience when we discover how the right tool not only makes a job easier but also makes us want to do more now that it's so much easier. The spindle method is just one such technique.

The roadmap of this book covers the what, how, and why:

What—What the spindle method is and how it works with the biology of pome fruits.

How – Ways you can adapt it to your garden rather than a large monoculture orchard

Why—The reasons it matters, and will become your next favorite garden perennial plant.

As a retired Waldorf school gardening and high school science teacher, I can't resist bringing in sidebars called "**Side Shoots**" to give you further scientific and historical notes that round out the story of apple growing as an art and science though the ages. (If you are interested in the espalier method, check out my webinar "Espalier Made Easy" at https://www.manzanitatlc.com/course,

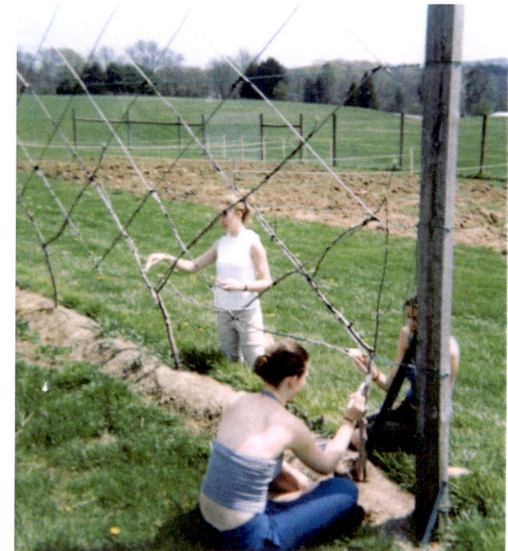

Belgian Fence Espalier getting getting a bark treatment in the Kimberton Waldorf school garden

One of my school garden classes that taught me that growing gardeners is my greatest joy

Apples 101: Leading Thoughts and Terminology

Some Leading Thoughts

Apple trees are large, woody plants that originated in forests where they had to compete for light. A hundred-plus years ago, an orchard was commonly planted in a grid with trees on a 20-by-20-foot square pattern. This plan means cultivating 100 trees per acre. These trees could spend 8 to 12 years getting established and another 30 to 60 years producing fruit before declining over the following decades. This layout also allowed a team of horses to pull a wagon and other equipment between the rows. Labor was cheaper back then, and tall ladders were required to work the trees. This layout was called "standard" and often used seedling trees as the rootstock to graft "improved" varieties on.

For many folks, this approach remains the standard orchard, but not for commercial growers today. Nearly all commercial growers have switched to variations on the spindle method described in this book; this method produces a plantation that looks more like a vineyard, with more than 1,000 trees per acre supported on trellises like grapevines. Yet backyard gardeners remain largely unfamiliar with the many advantages the small spindle format offers.

This is where apple gardening comes in. As this book will show, in the space of one big old tree, you can have a dozen little easy-to-manage trees yielding a couple bushels every month over a six-month period. Folks concerned about climate change understand the need for decarbonization. Locally grown apples are part of the answer.

Don't feel bad if you haven't heard about this before. I've been a certified arborist since 2012, and many arborists were unfamiliar with the method until recently. In early 2025 I gave a talk at the International Society of Arboriculture–Rocky Mountain Chapter's conference on "**What to Do About That Big Ol' Apple Tree**" to teach arborists from four Western states. My experience is that professional tree workers often do one of two things when it comes to apple trees: either treat them like any other ornamental tree or say, "We don't do fruit trees." In my talk, I suggested they might want to be able to offer information about the spindle method for folks who want to learn the most efficient way to grow apples. But the method remains known mostly by professional growers only.

Does the spindle method work on stone fruits like peaches, plums, or cherries? Not really. Although some good dwarfing cherry rootstocks come close to the spindle system, as you shall see in this book, the spindle method works because apples are a special kind of fruit. That leads to terminology, below. But like everything in biology, the apple is wonderful and fascinating.

Some Terminology

To understand the training and pruning necessary for the spindle method of apple growing, we'll need some common terminology, kind of like learning a new language. Some folks can hold an unknown word in their mind like a mathematician holds X as the unknown variable, only later to discover the answer and perhaps later still discover why it matters. So here are some terms that we'll unpack further as we go along.

Pome Fruits: Includes apples, pears, quince, and others.

Inferior Ovary: Refers to how the actual seed-bearing fruit is the apple's core, and the part we eat is actually modified wood.

Woody Fruit: My term for this specialized kind of fruit originating from modified wood, which lends itself to storability.

Plant Economy: How resources are limited, for example, how more fruits mean less shoots, and how wood energy is diverted into fruits.

Espalier: An ancient technique for training fruit trees, often in geometric, flat, or three-dimensional forms.

Apical Dominance: A trait found in forest trees whereby the uppermost bud or shoot releases a regulatory hormone that influences the tree's form.

Leader: A strongly growing vegetative branch that rapidly thickens into a permanent woody structure.

Central Leader: Also known as the Christmas tree form, whereby a given leader becomes the central trunk of a tree.

Secondary Scaffold Branches: Side shoots that form on large standard trees with a diameter that reaches 50% or more of that of the main trunk(s) (central leaders).

Lateral: A side-shoot branch that **hangs down** covered in fruit with little vegetation.

Spur: A very short lateral with flower buds and not much vegetative growth or extension.

Bud: Located at the base of every leaf, may contain a flower or a vegetative shoot. Every branch was once a bud or seed.

Bevel Cut: A renewal pruning technique exclusive to the spindle method; described on page 38.

Rootstock: Special rootstock cultivars are essential to success in the spindle system. See pages 41-45

Final Introductory Note

Especially in apples, *upward growth tends toward the vegetative* phase, which reenergizes the tree. Whereas *downward growth tends toward the reproductive* or fruiting phase, which disperses energy away from the tree in the form of growing fruit and seed. This fact underlies espalier and spindle methods, in which the gardener and the tree work together to create a beautiful harmony between form and fruit. As much as I love the espalier method, the spindle method of growing apples is better for most people. As I show in my webinar "Espalier Made Easy" (see https://www.manzanitatlc.com/course), the spindle method can be thought of as creating an informal single cordon with long laterals, rather than the tidy short spurs of espalier method. And if the espaliered tree is let go with several years of neglect, it loses its beautiful form; reestablishing it is usually too much for most gardeners. But the spindle method is far more forgiving and able to recover from a few years of neglect with pruning using the bevel cut.

INTRODUCTION

Why the Best Time to Plant a Tree Is Not Always 20 Years Ago

It's natural to become invested in something planted years ago. Yet if the plant was a poor choice at the time—because of location, variety, size—those problems don't go away. They just grow bigger.

One community I worked with had planted apple trees following the older standard system 20 years before, as a program for community engagement with folks of differing ages and abilities. For a time, this system went well. Yet as the trees grew bigger and taller, the ease of including volunteers became more limited, and the orchard's productivity became more inconsistent—in short, unmanageable. Big trees mean big problems.

I started converting the orchard over to the spindle method, and the benefits were obvious just two years later. With just a tenth of the orchard following spindle method, that tenth began outproducing the other 90%. It was also way more accessible, easier to maintain, and people-friendly, with little need for ladders.

I had been familiar with the spindle method previously, yet I had always thought of it as a commercial system geared for large-scale growers. But when a neighbor put in 20 acres following the spindle method, and I saw how quickly the apple trees got going, I found the courage to start on this conversion.

Oh, would that we had started with the spindle method in the first place!

Twenty years goes by quicker than you might think. Do you really want your volunteers going up ladders, or would you rather they stay on the ground? Yes, you can find it hard to take out older underperforming trees and replace them with spindle trees. But when you do it—you'll wonder why you didn't do it sooner. Other than "20 years ago," then, the next best time to plant a tree is as soon as possible, following a plan for long-term success, flexibility, and manageability. For that orchard conversion, I planted the new spindle trees following conventional guidelines. But I have since found planting in trios to be easier for most garden settings. In the next chapter, I share more about the trio spindle method, along with suggested trio combinations to help you navigate the overwhelming apple variety choices by focusing on season and types.

The Advantages of Spindle Trees

Although it has many aspects in common with other techniques (such as columnar, espalier, etc.), the spindle method pulls apple growing together in its simplest form, with many advantages.

Early Fruiting
Spindle trees start bearing fruit sooner than larger trees, depending on the **rootstock** and size of the nursery tree—as early as the second year.

Space and Light Efficiency
Small trees allow for better light penetration, which means higher quality and color. And you can grow more **varieties** in less space—creating a small apple garden instead of caring for one big old shady tree.

Accessibility
When you don't need a ladder, you'll get closer to your trees more often—saving time and effort. This approach is especially helpful for seniors and children or in public gardens.

Ease of Organic Care
All of these advantages mean that organic care practices—pruning, thinning, pest patrol, and application of bio remedies—become easier, more cost-effective, and thus more likely for you to get done in a timely manner.

Rediscovering the Superpower of Apples
What has made the apple a favorite for thousands of years is its **storability**—it provides foods that store well for colder seasons to warm both body and soul. The same quality—storability—means that apples **travel well** and thus can serve local food banks, schools, and neighborhood projects.

Reclaiming Regional Varieties
Whether you try growing specialty hard-cider varieties or culinary varieties for applesauce, pies, or pastries, small-scale growers can help preserve and spread **heirloom varieties** that are in danger of becoming lost.

Growing Neighborhood Connections
As your collection grows, you will begin sharing your passion with schools, community centers, churches, and more, creating neighborly connections and capacities. I find these connections to be the most satisfying fruit of horticulture—planting hope, growing gardeners, and strengthening neighborhoods.

The Limits of the Spindle Method

Long ago, we humans took the apple tree from the forest and created orchards. Later gardeners took the apple tree from the orchard and made smaller fruit gardens using espalier techniques. Today, the state-of-the-art spindle technique is the most efficient way to grow apples.

With each step in domestication (really a mutual relationship between us and the apple), we become more dependent upon one another.

But just as everything about a small spindle tree is easier and more accessible, so too is the **potential damage caused by grazing animals,** both wild and domestic. **Fencing** around a spindle orchard is essential because the trees are so accessible. Also, smaller trees will need s**upport structures** to carry the fruit load throughout their lifespan of 20 to 30 years. These small trees belong in a garden (or "guard-in").

Yet the legacy of growing large apple trees remains in many landscapes, leaving people scratching their heads about what these huge trees need and how to provide it. Seldom have I seen fruit trees function well as both a shade tree and a food source.

This book teaches the spindle method, whereby small size is achieved by grafting on to **specially selected rootstocks** that induce earlier fruiting and make for a smaller mature tree. Such trees appear more like bushes—or, when viewed on a large scale, more like a vineyard. Rather than seeing this as human manipulation of nature, we'll see how it works *with* the unique biology of the pome fruit rather than merely imposing the gardener's will upon it.

Now is the time to start **planning** your new spindle apple garden.

The Spindle tree looks more like a bush, with weeping lateral branches laden with fruit.

Shrinking Resources Prompt More Expertise

As demands on our time, space, and resources increase, we modify our techniques to best accommodate our circumstances. **This is how the spindle method developed.**

Bigger is not always better when it comes to the time required for moving ladders to pick and prune. Also, the amount of shadow cast by large trees pushes the best fruit-ripening regions up the tree and out of reach, further reducing efficiency and quality. The shrinking of trees and refining of techniques, in combination with specialized equipment, have together done a lot to reshape the business of commercial spindle orchards.

Forgive me for referring to the realm of the commercial grower. It's mainly because commercial apple growers are currently **the main practitioners of the spindle method.** When adapting the spindle method to your garden, you can use what works for you—and leave out what doesn't. These might include machinery, spray programs, large plantations, and support structures. The needs of the commercial grower, compared to the amateur grower, do not support an apple-to-apples comparison. (Pun intended.) Yet here's a takeaway for you: **New York's apple growers went from producing 0% of the nation's organic apples to producing 5% by using the spindle method for production and better environmental stewardship.**

Commercial growers have access to quality wholesale trees grown especially for the Spindle technique on specialty rootstocks

Most apples on the market today are grown using the spindle method. A wholesale supply chain supports the commercial spindle growers; it is largely unknown to amateur growers, much like the method itself.

You may have noticed several new varieties of apples on the market. These became available because commercial growers have been able to bring new trees into production faster, which benefits their return on investment.

Hobbyists and small-scale growers are often able to grow heirloom and other specialty varieties that may be unsuitable for commercial growers, often because these varieties bruise easily or don't store or travel well. In a later section, I'll highlight some varieties to pique your interest for your apple garden.

Side Shoot 1

Origin of the Apple
Along the Silk Road . . .

Long ago and far away, travelers made the arduous journey between the Far East and the European West to exchange valuable goods along routes that later came to be known collectively as the Silk Road.

Silk is a textile with such extraordinary properties that modern material science engineers still study it. Yet back then, silk production was a guarded trade that included partnerships among gardeners, weavers, and a species of domesticated moth. The moth's chrysalis is constructed of a single long fiber, which can be unraveled, spun, and woven into textiles of extreme beauty, function, and value.

So great was its value that travelers found it worthwhile to make these long, difficult journeys to exchange valuable goods for it in ancient marketplaces—spurring not only economic exchanges but cultural exchanges among different peoples, languages, and perspectives.

Imagine the challenges that long-distance travel posed so many centuries ago, including steep terrain, weather, the provisioning of food and water, and more. Caravans of animals, some needed for food and others used as beasts of burden, were required to make such a journey.

In the forests of what is today Kazakhstan grew a fruit well adapted to the hot summers and cold winters that followed a very different era in Earth's climate history: the last ice age. That fruit is the humble apple.

Apples traveled well and gradually came with people all over the world, providing strength and sweetness through the seasons. Like the valuable silk, apples went on to become one of the most valuable traded cultural items. In 2019 the global apple market was valued at $78 billion per year, versus silk, valued at around $20 billion per year.

Although apples are found throughout northern temperate latitudes, select cultivars were identified long ago and were propagated using cuttings and grafting as well as seeds.

Since apples are open-pollinated plants (see Side Shoot 3), they are open to evolving ever new varieties as characteristics are mixed in seeds because of flowering. Hence today we have thousands of apple varieties with complex heritages that followed the early varieties from the Far East to Rome, Europe, the Americas, and throughout the world.

Part of the special qualities of apples has to do with the unique biology of pome fruits, which I touch on in other Side Shoots.

How the Spindle Technique Changes Tree Architecture

"Architecture" is the term used in high-density orchards to describe the spacing in rows, between rows, and for height. As mentioned already, older standard orchards consisted of large self-supporting trees, often planted 20 feet apart in each direction—for 100 trees per acre, with trees standing 16 to 30 feet tall.

Modern orchards look more like vineyards, featuring more than 1,000 trees per acre, with trees planted every 3 to 6 feet in rows 10 to 12 feet apart. Variations on layout or architecture are intended to maximize space efficiency and to accommodate machinery.

Often older orchards used standard central-leader trees (see Apples 101), with a main trunk followed by secondary scaffold branches leading to fruit-bearing laterals just on the periphery. These trees can take 6 to 12 years to establish, followed by 20 to 40 years of production, which in turn is followed by decline, associated with shadow, disease, and lessening productivity.
The spindle method radically changes all this by reducing the tree to one single trunk, or "spindle," with no secondary scaffold branches, and encouraging the apple tree to go straight to producing as many as 20 weeping lateral branches covered with flowers and later fruit, all within easy reach of humans and sunlight.

This form basically gives you a mature, or heavily fruiting, tree in around six years—yet comes with the cost of requiring a permanent support structure. East of the Mississippi, growers call this the "tall spindle" method, while out West the system tends to be smaller.

Small-scale growers can plant self-supporting trios and save the cost of big trellis systems while integrating these apple gardens into more diversified garden landscapes.

In the next chapter, consider the easiest trio to start with.

Older Standard orchard architecture

High-density plantings using 1,000+ trees per acre on dwarfing rootstocks are designed around equipment, labor, and light efficiency.

DESIGNING YOUR COLLECTION

Advantages of Planting in Trios

Rather than planting in long rows, plant in groups of three, between 24 and 48 inches apart, and create a common support pillar.

Planting in trios has many advantages:
- Trios avoid the need to build an expensive, long trellis wall, which limits movement around your garden.
- The support structure is mutually supportive.
- The trio system makes it easier to keep track of varieties when you lose a label—and you will.
- Trios allow for better pollination for more fruit.
- The system is very scalable. You can have just one trio or many to produce just as much as you need or want.
- You can have three trios, separately ripening in August, September, and October, to spread out the harvest.
- You can spread them out to avoid a monoculture look (think of an unending field of corn).
- You can more easily add or subtract trees as needed.
- Trees like company in mini groves.

Trios can also be arranged by use, such as:

- Season of ripening: July, August, September, October, November
- Storing varieties for use in December, January, February, and March
- Culinary varieties for summer, fall, and winter
- Hard or sweet cider types
- Small bite-sized or edible crabapples
- Disease-resistant, easier to grow varieties
- Regional favorites
- Whatever combination you'd like

Support structure for trio 24-36" apart

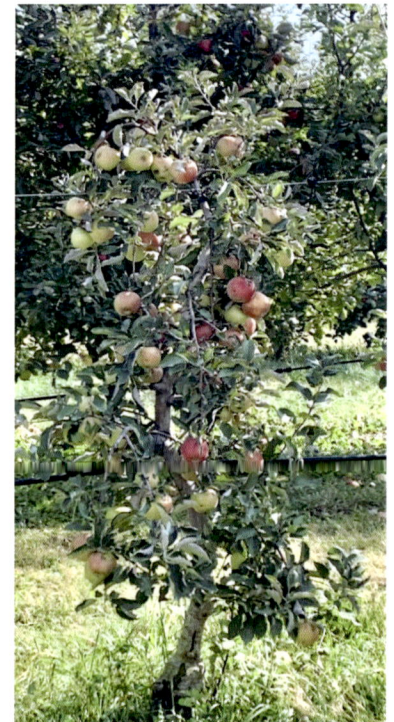

Rather than rows try 3 of these together

So Many Apple Varieties

As so many apple varieties are available, you can find it overwhelming to know where to start. So I've recommended the first trio in this section as the place to start. It will give you disease-free apples in August and September while you gain confidence in caring for your spindle trees. The section after this one covers training after piquing your interest here with the possible varieties you might choose.

Stories Behind Every Variety

As you explore the many varieties of apples, you'll come across information that might make you stop considering that variety . . . but keep an open mind. I've grown less than 5% of the more than 2,000 varieties available, and I've come to realize that varieties that are really not worth growing were discarded long ago. There are reasons why collectors are still passionately sharing obscure varieties.

For example, my family and I were living in Sonoma County in California during the centennial celebration for the Gravenstein apple, circa 1990. From the 1880s, a local pie, sauce, and juice industry grew up there around the Gravenstein apple—an industry that has since been overshadowed by the wine industry.

Very few people still grow the Gravenstein apple, but the variety remains the best apple for about two weeks in August. It is the official apple of Denmark and originated in northern Germany in the 1600s. Commercial growers find it too niche to bother with. Yet it's not uncommon for breeders to go back to these heirloom varieties for breeding purposes. You'll find it in my other honorable mentions in Trio 10 below, culinary apples.

A cooperative American breeding program affiliated with Purdue, Rutgers, and Illinois universities names its varieties with "pri" somewhere in the name to indicate their origin as quality, hardy apples bred with some natural disease-resistant characteristics, such as Pristine and so on.

Fourteen Trio Suggestions

1. **Easy No-Spray:** Pristine, William's Pride, Liberty
2. Another **Easy No-Spray:** CrimsonCrisp, SnowSweet, Enterprise
3. **Early Season:** Yellow Transparent, Beauty of Bath, Dayton
4. **Main Season:** Jonagold, Sweet Sixteen, Ambrosia
5. **Late Season:** Winesap, King David, Gold Rush
6. Another **Late Season:** Pomme Gris, Newton Pippin, Roxbury Russet
7. **Multi-Season Bite-Sized:** Transcendent, Chestnut, Pipsqueak
8. **More Bite-Sized:** Centennial, Dolgo, Wickson
9. **Yet More Bite-Sized:** Kinder Crisp, Pixie Crunch, Northland
10. **Culinary:** Bramley's, Caville Blanc, Granny Smith+
11. **Hard Cider:** Golden Russet, Baldwin, Porter's Perfection
12. **Hard Cider/Multipurpose:** Golden Russet, Baldwin, Porter's Perfection
13. **Low Chill:** Sundowner, Kandil Sinap, Winter Banana+
14. **Regional:** Co. Orange, Early Joe, Dolores River Sorbet

Thanks, and credit go to Cummins Nursery for giving permission to use their photos in these descriptions..

1. Easy No-Spray Trio

Pristine—Photo Credit MV

William's Pride—Photo Credit Cummins

Liberty—Photo Credit Cummins

This is the trio I recommend you start with, or the one to plant if you are planning just one trio.

These varieties start off the season with the easiest apples possible while leaving you free to attend to all the other chores you have in late summer through early fall.

Each of these modern selections resulted from careful natural breeding and testing. "Resistance" does not mean immunity; it just suggests varying degrees of resistance to some common fungal or bacterial diseases. For the most part, these varieties can produce a good clean crop without spraying. Yet this quality does not mean they are pest-resistant. Organic growers use a variety of sprays for pest control and for health. Growers in more humid climates find their apples suffer more from rust and scab diseases. In fact, I came to love this trio when I moved from California to Pennsylvania, where I discovered more apple diseases and pests than I ever knew existed.

Pristine

A crisp, tender, fresh-eating yellow apple that ripens in August—perfect for getting your season going early. One of the best early yellow apples. I've found its early-ripening season useful for summer youth programs and activities. (More on that later.)

William's Pride

Another fresh-eating apple that ripens in August. It tends to ripen not all at once but over a two-week period. This characteristic teaches you how to be more sensitive to when to harvest. When an apple is ready to pick, the stem stays connected to the fruit. Test it by gently lifting on the fruit; when ripe, it comes free in your hand with the stem attached. If the stem tears off, it wasn't ready to pick!

Liberty

The champion of apples for organic growers because it has the greatest disease-resistance profile of any apple variety. I found this a perfect multipurpose apple in my school garden in the warm, humid, disease-prone climate of the Mid-Atlantic region, where as a busy teacher I didn't have time to get to every task right at the start of the school year. Ripens in late September.

2. Another Easy No-Spray Trio

CriimsonCrisp™ Photo Credit Cummins

Breeding programs often patent the products of their work and apply to use the registered trademark (®) symbol. These steps help pay for the research and efforts for 20 years from filing. To further extend their return on investment they occasionally will file a trademark application to use the trademark (™) symbol, which protects a particular trade name without time limit. These are two different things. Pink Lady®, originally known as Cripp's Pink—its unregistered name—is one such trade-named apple that you may see in markets. Commercial growers pay a licensing fee to the owner to use the trade name when selling the produce.

CrimsonCrisp™

Originally known as Coop-39; comes from a region where scab is a challenge. Ripens in late September. In areas with high pressures from cedar apple rust and fire blight, this variety might not be the best choice. Delightfully crisp and delicious.

SnowSweet®

Comes out of the University of Minnesota's apple breeding program; such fruits should catch the attention of growers in colder regions like USDA Zone 5 or colder. A hardy late-season apple ripening in late October. Slow to brown after slicing, it makes a good apple for fruit salads or dehydrating.

SnowSweet® Photo Credit Cummins

Enterprise

Ripens in late September and has a great disease-resistance profile. Some folks find the skin a bit tough, yet this toughness may contribute to its resistance to disease and some pests. Like other tart apples, it is a good pie apple. It was always disease-free for us in Pennsylvania's Zone 6.

Enterprise Credit Cummins

10

3. Early Season Trio

Yellow Transparent July

Beauty of Bath August

Dayton Mid-August

Unlike commercial growers, in your apple garden you can grow special-purpose varieties that are seldom grown commercially, typically because they bruise easily or go soft too quickly for the supply chain's travel time. The benefit of early-ripening varieties first occurred to me when I was donating trees to local youth educational gardens. What they needed were varieties that ripen during the summer.

As a former garden teacher, I appreciate having enough timely tasty produce on hand for children to experience. This context is where early-ripening varieties can really shine.

Yellow Transparent Perrine

A larger earlier version of the White Transparent apple that was discovered by D. B. Perrine in Illinois. It is winter hardy and is free of most diseases but is susceptible to fire blight. Makes a good smooth applesauce. Ripens mid- to late July.

Beauty of Bath

A summer apple good for fresh eating or cooking. Was popular in England before commercial varieties displaced it in the markets. Good disease resistance. Like other summer apples, it is not a keeper (does not store well).

Dayton

Another summer low-spray variety with good disease resistance for fresh use. Tolerates hot climate better than most apples. Crisp sweet-tart flavor.

Side Shoot 2

What Are Sports?

Don't be surprised if your supposed Fuji apple doesn't look the same as someone else's . . .

'Regular' Fuji Photo Credit Cummins

Occasionally a branch on a tree has fruit that looks different from all the others—it's called a "sport." Often it has different coloration, size, or other distinct characteristics. These can be propagated vegetatively by grafting and can be identified as a variant or sport of the parent tree and variety. There over two dozen sports of Red Delicious.

Commercial nurseries often seek these sports out, as the patent propagation rights can start and run for another 20 years. We used to have an old Red Delicious sport from the 1960s that was fantastic—along with the five prominent ribs at the base so characteristic of the Red Delicious, it had a great texture and flavor and was resistant to Cedar Apple Rust. Yet the Red Delicious is a favorite apple variety to hate because it displaced so many other regional heirloom varieties. But it has always scored high in taste tests.

How sports occur is somewhat of a mystery. That's even more reason to pay attention to names and labels, as these variants often put the main named variety into a different class of character than the original.

We had a block of Fuji trees that never ripened in Zone 6 that we took out. They were just too much work for no fruit. I wish I had known about the early-ripening sport of Fuji known as Beni-Shogun, or Heisei Fuji. So before you say, "Fujis are hard to grow," maybe a variant or sport would work better in your region.

Again, planting in trios can help you keep track of varieties, including various sports, especially when labels get lost. Take pictures that include the labels and make notes in journals or computer files so you can explain why your sports look different from the regular strains.

'Beni' Fuji Sport Photo Credit Cummins

4. Main Season Trio

Jonagold Late Sept.

Sweet Sixteen Mid- Sept.

Ambrosia Late Sept.

There are a lot of choices in the main season category. This trio is a backyard trio suitable for USDA Zones 5 through 8 with excellent fresh-eating, cider, and cooking qualities that you'll love.

Jonagold

A large crisp apple ripening in the latter part of the main season. Combines the best of Jonathan and Golden Delicious. It tends toward , meaning it crops heavy one year and light the next. This alternating pattern can be addressed by thinning 30 to 50% of the crop on a heavy year to save the trees energy for the next year (see later section on "Years 5 to 20: Mature Tree Maintenance").

Sweet Sixteen

Also a cold-hardy type that came out of the University of Minnesota breeding program. Ripens mid-season; is crisp, sweet, and slow to oxidize. Easy to grow and popular among organic growers.

Ambrosia

An excellent dessert apple that is competing with Honeycrisp and Pink Lady in the markets. Good as fruit salad apple or slicer because it's slow to brown. Good baking apple that stores for three months.

Side Shoot 3

Pollination and Ploidy Types

Apples set more fruit when they have more varieties of pollen and pollinators around.

In the world of plants, flowering plants are evolutionary newcomers that have developed relationships with various insects and animals that aid their success in survival and reproduction and enhance their contribution to their ecological community.

A wide variety of insect pollinators visit apple blossoms and in the process transfer pollen from one variety to another, initiating trees' formation of seed and fruit. This variety includes honeybees plus dozens of native bee species as well.

Planting in trios helps ensure better, more consistent fruit set because the more varieties of flowers there are, the better fruit sets. Blooming happens in **four seasons, from early to late (see trios 1 to 4),** such that an early 1 bloomer may not provide adequate pollen at the right time for a late blooming 4 variety. In cold climates you might benefit from group 4, the later blooming varieties. The more the merrier.

Botanically, most apples are considered **diploid,** *meaning they have* **two sets of chromosomes.** *Some of the very large apples, like JonaGold, have* **three sets of chromosomes.** *These* **triploids don't provide good pollen for other varieties,** *so they benefit from the pollen of at least two other diploid types. Good nurseries that specialize in fruit trees will list the "ploidy" type—diploid or triploid—in their plants and catalogs.*

In general, lack of fruit-set is often less of a problem than too much fruit!

In a later section I describe **thinning** *strategies for the backyard gardener, as the task is an important summer chore needed for good success and general plant health. Commercial growers use chemical thinners to reduce heavy cropping and encourage better-sized fruits, but most gardeners simply thin any excess fruit by hand to promote plant vigor.*

5. Late Season Trio

Late-season apples develop their best qualities after harvesting. Traditionally, apples were stored in cellars, barns, or other outbuildings for use during the winter months. These three varieties were favorites in our orchard in Pennsylvania.

Winesap Oct-Nov

Winesap

A reliable, beloved American heirloom variety with good disease resistance. Like other triploid varieties, it needs at least two other diploid pollinators to set fruit well (see Side Shoot 3). It is good eaten fresh, baked, sauced, and pressed for cider. Stores well for three months or more.

King David Oct-Nov

King David

A neighbor in Pennsylvania who grew more than 300 apple varieties introduced this one to me as one of his favorites, and now I know why. A highly flavored dessert apple that has good disease resistance and productivity and is easy to grow. Awesome apple for pies, sauce, and cider. Another American heirloom variety. Stark Bros. introduced it 1902. Diploid.

Gold Rush Oct-Nov

Gold Rush

Although cold-hardy, needs Zone 5 or warmer to completely ripen late in the season. Has a great flavor and is very popular among organic growers due to its good disease resistance; yet is somewhat susceptible to Cedar Apple Rust. Diploid.

6. Another Late Season Trio

You seldom see russet-type apples in the market because appearance is everything. Due to their rough skin, russet types don't polish up with waxes the way smooth-skinned types do. But they are firm, solid, satisfying apples and deserve a place with home gardeners who store their apples. These three all store well.

Pomme Gris

A favorite of Thomas Jefferson, this heirloom is usually greenish with a slight gray appearance, sometimes with a red blush on the sunny side, and is covered with a fine, rough surface typical of russet types. Best used as a stored dessert apple with excellent flavor and aroma. Diploid (see Side Shoot 3).

Newtown Pippin

Another favorite of Jefferson, Benjamin Franklin, and George Washington, the Newtown Pippin is a late-season variety with a sweet-tart flavor and a slight russet surface. Although it is often eaten fresh after storing, its popularity is more associated with baking and cidermaking. Diploid.

Roxbury Russet

Almost inedible when first harvested but sweetens in storage. Stores well, which made it one of America's more popular varieties in the early 1600s. Excellent baking and cider apple. Like other triploid varieties, it needs at least two other diploid pollinators to set fruit well.

Pomme Gris Photo Credit Cummins

Newtown Pippin PhotoCredit Cummins

Roxbury Russet Oct. Credit Cummins

7. Multi-Season Bite-Sized Trio

Transcendent Crab August

One of the great joys of gardening is being able to offer a taste sensation full of life, crisp texture, aroma, and complex flavor straight from the garden. This joy is appreciated by folks of all ages, but especially children. When you cultivate this trio, you can enjoy these treats through summer, fall, and winter.

Transcendent Crab

A cold-hardy, heat-tolerant variety like many crabapple varieties. Like most early ripening apples, does not keep long and is best enjoyed right away. Has an orange skin with a yellow flesh. Although susceptible to fire blight, it has been used in breeding programs. Triploid (see Side Shoot 3).

Chestnut Crab August

Chestnut Crab

Large for a crabapple, at around two inches; will change your opinion that "crabs" are just for wildlife. Great for fresh use as well as cider, baking, sauce, and jelly. Cold-hardy, heat-tolerant, with good disease resistance. The trees weeping form makes it a popular flowering ornamental with fruit as a highlight. Diploid.

Pipsqueak October

Pipsqueak

A small dessert apple with a long stem that ripens in early October. Another great fresh-eating crabapple type. Under two inches, but full of flavor. Try rolling in cinnamon sugar and baking whole. Hardy to Zone 4. Possibly a seedling of Frostbite™, originally MN447.

8. More Bite-Sized Trio

Continuing our theme of good things that come in tiny packages, here's another trio of edible crabapples.

Centennial
A sweet little mid-August crabapple that is very cold-hardy and heat-tolerant. Easy to grow. Great for snacking, sauce, or baking. A perfect little summer apple for children or adults who are young at heart. Developed at the University of Minnesota in 1957, when they were developing hardy apples of promise by crossing Dolgo and Wealthy varieties. Named in honor of Minnesota's centennial year of statehood. Resistant to scab and fire blight.

Centennial August Photo Credit Cummins

Dolgo
A Russian crabapple known for its cold hardiness and disease resistance to fire blight, powdery mildew, and cedar apple rust. I first encountered it as a pollinator apple on the edge of an orchard. It was brought to North Dakota by Niels Hanson after he collected its seeds in Siberia in 1897. One of the few self-fertilizing varieties of apple, meaning it does not need a pollinator. Was planted as a wildlife and ornamental plant in the high plains of the United States. Makes a bitter-sharp cider and a pink applesauce and jelly. Diploid (see Side Shoot 3).

Dolgo August PhotoCredit Cummins

Wickson Crabapple
Developed by West Coast apple breeder Albert Etter, who has also encouraged an interest in red-fleshed apple varieties. This October-ripening variety has a red skin and yellow flesh with an intense sharp-sweet flavor that works in jellies but really shines in cider. (Dozens of rare heirloom cider varieties are beloved by microbreweries that blend varieties to achieve unique flavors.)

Wickson Crabapple Oct. Credit Cummins

9. Yet More Bite-Sized Trio

Kinder Crisp September

Commercial growers have always catered to big fruits. Yet I find I can't eat a whole apple these days and much prefer just a few bites of something snappy and flavorful than too much of something perhaps less delectable. Quality first, then quantity!

Kinder Crisp

A recent offspring (2012) of HoneyCrisp yet smaller. Very hardy in Zones 3 and 4. Very crisp and sweet. Ripens in early September. Mildly susceptible to scab and rust, so it won't do well in humid regions with those diseases. Diploid (see Side Shoot 3).

Pixie Crunch

A crisp, tasty small apple; good school garden variety. Fairly resistant to scab and fire blight but somewhat susceptible to cedar apple rust and powdery mildew. Originally called Coop 33, emerged from the Purdue/Rutgers/Illinois breeding program in 1978. Diploid.

Pixie Crunch Late September

Northland Crabapple

A cold-hardy crabapple with yellow flesh tinged with red; ripens in August. Excellent dessert apple. Great in blends of apple jelly or applesauce. Released by the University of Minnesota in 1957. Susceptible to scab and fire blight. Diploid

Northland Crab August

A Renaissance of Cider

*Juice made from fresh apples is called **cider**. Allowed to ferment, it becomes **hard cider**. When hard cider is distilled it becomes **applejack,** or **apple brandy**.*

Colonial America drank more cider than wine or beer. Then in the 19th century, more grain was grown and beer production expanded, and Cider faded into the background. In the 20th century, wine production took off following the invention of the grape harvester; commercial wine production took off particularly in California.

Now in the 21st century we're seeing a renaissance of home brewers and microbreweries involved in beer and cider production. Along with this rebirth came the hunt for heirloom varieties that were once especially favored for the sharp dry distinctive flavors preferred in hard cider.

My grandmother, Celia Chase Mason, grew up on a three-generation family farm with a cider mill that served the community around Buda, Illinois, from 1840 to 1906. The Masons were teetotalers who only favored nonalcoholic fresh cider. But my Uncle Ivan told me about the hard cider and applejack that were popular on his side of the family as well as in many rural communities before, during, and after Prohibition. Hard cider has 5 to 18% alcohol content; distillation via steam or freezing brings the content to 20 to 40% alcohol to create an apple brandy, sometimes called applejack.

Look for custom cider mills in your area where you can bring your fruit for pressing, processing, and canning.

Bramley's Seedling Sept.

Calville Blanc October

Granny Smith November

10. Culinary Trio

Most culinary apples are generally not eaten fresh, so we don't see them in American markets. These really shine in pies, pastries, and sauces. Many varieties are praised for keeping their shape and texture, while others cook into a fine puree. An apple grower could find a niche market selling directly to specialty bakeries.

Bramley's Seedling

A favorite pie apple in England, where the city of Nottingham puts on an annual Bramley festival. Cooks down to fluff; some pastry makers prefer an apple that holds its shape better. Great for folks with tender teeth. Also good in cider blends. Resistant to scab. Like other triploids it needs two diploids for good pollination (see Side Shoot 3). Grows in Zones 4 and 5 or higher.

Calville Blanc

The favorite French culinary apple. A lumpy full-figured apple you wouldn't expect to see in the market; its beauty shines in pastries. Has more vitamin C than an orange. Rather acidic at harvest but mellows in storage. Diploid.

Granny Smith

The Australian culinary apple. When allowed to fully ripen, it is a dual-purpose apple variety with that green-apple candy flavor that makes it popular for fresh eating. Like a good tomato, nothing beats homegrown. Diploid. Zones 6 or 7 or warmer. Ripens in November.

Other honorable mentions in the culinary category include these:

Baldwin, Belle de Boskoop, Mutsu, Rome Beauty, Rhode Island Greening, Wolf River, Prairie Spy, Spitzenburg, Spy Gold, Lamb Abby Pearman, and Smokehouse.

Early summer culinary apples include the following:

Gravenstein, Duchess of Oldenburg, Almata (red-fleshed), Summer Rambo, and Yellow Transparent.

11. Hard Cider Trio

Most sweet fruits have been used in fermented beverages. Bitterness as a flavor has fallen out of most modern cuisine—but it is sought out in distilled products. Many people are rediscovering plant compounds such as bitters and other phytochemical compounds found in the skin and various colors of fruits and vegetables. Many cider varieties are so bitter that they are not suitable for eating fresh but are used exclusively for cider. Old cider makers called this spectrum of flavors "sharp and sweet"; these qualities were traditionally blended to give complex flavor to fresh cider and hard cider alike. Both Old and New World apples include dozens of favorite heirloom cider apple varieties.

Harry Masters

A small bittersweet type from England used only in hard-cider blends; also known as the Port Wine apple variety. Tolerates hot but not too humid climate. Good in Zones 5 through 8. Fruit drops when ripe in September. Not a keeper apple. It is tip-bearing—which means it usually bears fruit not on short spurs but on the ends of last year's branches. As a result, it responds well to the spindle method of fruiting laterals. A weak grower that requires using a stronger dwarf rootstock (see later chapter on rootstocks). Diploid (see Side Shoot 3).

Redfield

Also called Geneva Red, a newer cider variety—slightly red-fleshed, disease-resistant, late-season, sharp-flavor—that is very hardy in Zones 3 through 7.

Franklin

Named after Franklin County, Vermont, where it was discovered in 2008. A bitter-sharp cider type, yet sweet enough to eat fresh. Hardy in Zones 3 through 7 with good disease resistance. Diploid.

Harry Masters Late Sept.

Redfield November

Franklin October

12. Hard Cider/Multipurpose

Here's a dual-purpose trio, good for general use as storage apples and also popular in cider blends.

Golden Russett

A favorite multi-use American heirloom keeping apple from the 1700s. Remains crisp and sweet for around three months; good for baking, cider, and eating. Hardy to Zones 4 through 6. Diploid (see Side Shoot 3).

Baldwin

Another multipurpose American heirloom good for cider, baking, sauce, jelly, fresh eating, and storage. Named after Loammi Baldwin, second cousin to Johnny Appleseed. Triploid, so it needs two diploids to set fruit well.

Black Oxford

Another American heirloom and one of the favorite apples of New England's famous organic advocates, the late Michael Phillips. Cold-hardy, disease-resistant, tasty; good for baking, making sweet cider, and storing. Diploid.

Other multipurpose cider honorable mentions include these:

Ashmead's kernel, Roxbury Russet, Empire, Northern Spy, Cox's Orange Pippin, JonaGold, Chestnut Crab, Caville Blanc, Liberty, Egremont Russet, Reinette Zabergau, Grimes Golden, Hudson's Golden Gem, Spitzenburg Esopus, Newtown Pippin, Dared, MacIntosh, St. Edmund's Russet, Martha Crabapple, and Lamb Abby Pearmain.

Black Oxford November

13. Low Chill Trio

As mentioned in the first Side Shoot about the origin of apples, these trees evolved a strategy to deal with cold winters following the last Ice Age. This evolution includes a chemical that slowly degrades in the cold, acting like a delayed fuse for blooming and leafing out in spring. "Chill hours" describes the time needed below 45°; most apple tree varieties require from 400 to 600 chill hours. But for folks in Zone 8 or warmer, that's not going to happen. If you're in those zones, you can grow low-chill varieties. Mild zones have lots of soft subtropical fruit (think guavas, papayas, etc.). Grow these apples to add something crisp!

Sundowner®

An apple from the same breeder of Pink Lady® in Australia. Requires fewer than 300 chill hours; tolerates long, hot summers. Ripens in November. Crisp and tangy-sweet. Fresh, baking, and sauce apple that stores well for three months. Good for Zones 6 through 8. Diploid (see Side Shoot 3).

Kandil Sinap

An ancient exotic apple from Turkey that is easy to grow in Zones 5 through 8. Has an unusual, elongated shape. Tolerates heat and is fireblight resistant. Stores well up to three months. Needs fewer than 400 chill hours. Diploid.

Winter Banana

This variety was once represented by just a few trees planted in old orchards as a pollinator. Its mild flavor develops if allowed to fully ripen. Used in cider blends. Thin skin makes it unsuitable for commercial markets because it easily bruises. Requires fewer than 400 chill hours. Grows in Zones 4 through 8. Diploid

Other low-chill honorable mentions include these:

Anna (chill hours under 200), Golden Dorset (chill hours under 100), Ein Shemer (chill hours under 200, Zones 8 and 9).

Winter Banana October

14. Regional Trio

Most regions have heirloom favorites that you can find with a little research in your area, whether Western, Northeastern, Southern, or elsewhere. Here are three examples that were new to me upon moving to Colorado; they were preserved by the Montezuma Orchard Project. Other organizations include North American Fruit Explorers, Fedco, and the California Rare Fruit Growers.

Colorado Orange

Rescued from an old orchard in Colorado, it has that warm Colorado color in a blocky form. Late-ripening, multi-use keeping apple. Diploid (see Side Shoot 3).

Early Joe

Originally from New York around 1800 and later brought to Colorado, whose western slope is a good fruit-growing region with plenty of moisture. Diploid.

Dolores River Sorbet

A red-fleshed crabapple found along the Dolores River in southwest Colorado. Diploid

I'll post photos when they fruit!

Starting *Your* Apple Collection

The listed trios are just examples to get you thinking about curating your own collection. You can pursue other ways to identify the best candidates for your collection.

Local Growers: Find as many growers and amateur organizations as you can in your area and ask about their favorites, their greatest challenges, and what do they not recommend. Remember, you don't have the same needs commercial growers have, so you can take a path less traveled.

Disease Resistance: Find out what diseases are most common to your area, and consider varieties that have known resistance to these. The common ones include cedar apple rust, fire blight, powdery mildew, and scab.

Hardiness: Identify your USDA climate zone and choose varieties with suitable cold hardiness for your region.

Pollination Requirements: The more varieties you grow, the less pollination poses a problem. Commercial growers with large blocks of one apple variety sometimes must take certain measures to make sure they have adequate pollination. See Side Shoot 3.

Heat Tolerance: This is becoming more of an issue due to climate change, even in cool areas.

Ripening Season: Too much of a good thing can be a problem. You can spread out your ripening season by collecting the right mix of early-, middle-, and late-season varieties, as well as storing varieties.

Use: Most people think of apples as only a fresh-eating fruit. But culinary varieties for making pies, sauce, apple butter, and other baking used to be much more common. If you have a local custom cider mill, you can easily process apples for cider, which can in turn be frozen, fermented, or distilled as described in Side Shoot 4.

Other Collectible Varieties: The lists of heirloom varieties, red-fleshed varieties, regional varieties, and new varieties seem to grow every year. My recent passion is collecting small-sized varieties as well as early ripening varieties to share with summer youth gardening programs.

*　　*　　*

Many readers at this point might say, "**What about XYZ** and many hundreds of other great varieties?" I've left plenty of varieties for you to explore.

My focus in this book is to show how the spindle method allows you to grow 12 small trees in the space that one old standard tree used to require. With this method, using these or other trios, you're more likely to find the space, time, and skills to easily create your own apple collection as part of a renaissance in regional apple growing that benefits you, your family, and your neighbors far more than the challenges that come with big old apple trees.

PRUNING AND TRAINING

It All Starts with a Lead Shoot

Apples are plants with what is called **apical dominance**. This means the uppermost shoot (called a "**leader**") releases a hormone that holds the other shoots back, creating a natural order that arborists call "ordination." Apical dominance is a strategy that forest trees evolved to compete for light. On bigger trees, this growth order goes as follows: trunk—scaffold branches—laterals. In older orchard systems this form is called the "central leader" form. Yet the spindle method permits no scaffold branches. The central trunk is the only permanent scaffold, on which cascading laterals bear fruit; these are replaced when they grow to greater than around 40 to 60% of the trunk's diameter. **This method gives the spindle apple plant the appearance of a bush**. For reasons we'll go into later, only pome fruits like apples respond well to this spindle method—trees of stone fruits are different.

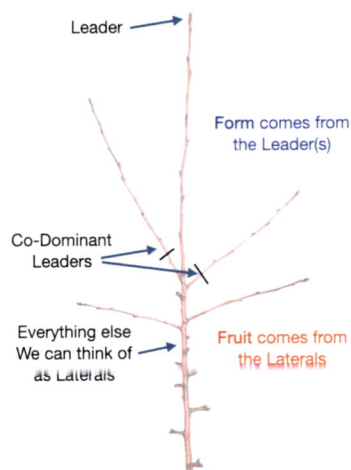

Leader →

Form comes from the Leader(s)

Co-Dominant Leaders →

Everything else We can think of → Fruit comes from as Laterals the Laterals

The spindle method's genius lies in **eliminating scaffold branches and having the leader form a simple trunk (the spindle) early on. In this way, the energy is redirected into the laterals, so *you get more fruit on smaller trees sooner*.** This means that in the mature spindle—after about six years—the height, via a leader, relaxes, and the energy is diverted into weeping laterals covered with fruit—leading the plant to form a kind of mature bush rather than a vigorous tree.

This effect is achieved using special dwarfing rootstocks (see next chapter for more on these). With the right rootstocks, you eliminate the middleman of scaffolding branches and go straight to the fruit-bearing laterals right off the main trunk. For commercial growers, this practice leads to high-density plantings. For noncommercial growers, you can develop what I call "apple gardening" versus cultivating plantation-style monocultures.

And this method greatly simplifies training and pruning!

Since the apple plant has only one leader, which becomes the trunk or spindle, everything else becomes laterals. That's where most of the training and pruning work occurs. Laterals should have a wide-angle attachment (see diagram on this page). If they have a narrow attachment, they may be codominant branches, especially if their diameter is 50% or larger of the diameter of the Leader. **These codominant ones should be cut out as soon as possible—**otherwise, they stimulate excess vegetative vigor rather than the early fruiting that comes from the weeping laterals that are so essential to the spindle technique (see the next page). The spindle system entails minimal pruning. Most of your focus will center on bending down lateral branches during the first half of summer, which encourages flower buds to form during the latter part of summer that can fruit next year, when the resulting fruit will bend the laterals naturally.

Three Branch Types: Leader, Codominant, and Laterals

Functionally, the apple tree has three types of branches. By diverting vegetative vigor from its upright-growing tendency toward heavily fruiting cascading laterals, we create a smaller, more mature form sooner. This practice does come at the cost of a support trellis, individual stakes, or the trio approach's pillar combination to keep the plants from falling over from the weight. So it helps to understand more about these branch types.

Leader: The tree has **just one central leade**r: the trunk or spindle. This is the largest woody structural element. During the first eight years, it is not strong enough to support all the laterals loaded with fruit and so needs extra support. Depending on the size of the initial tree, you may need up to four years to grow this central leader to the top of your support before bending it over like another lateral after it grows past the support.

Laterals: Most of your training focus during the first five to six years will be bending laterals down so they start producing flower buds during a critical window between July and August when these buds are set for the next growing season. As soon as fruit starts forming along these laterals, the weight of the fruit will do the bending for you. Lateral branches can vary in length from a short 1-inch spur to a 3-foot cascading lateral. If you sense a lot of vigor in a given plant, you can allow longer laterals and more fruit per year for that tree. Here are some targets for the total fruits per tree: year 1, up to 5; year 2, up to 20; year 3, up to 40; year 4, up to 70; year 5, up to 90. Starting around year 6 and beyond, you'll max out at around 20 lateral branches per tree and will begin replacing one or two laterals each year using the bevel cut technique (see Side Shoot 7).

Codominant — These branches in between leaders and laterals aspire to be leaders. Their diameter tends to be 50% or more of the diameter of the Leader, and they have a narrow branch attachment shaped like a *V* rather than the *L*-shape attachment of a true lateral. Codominants should be removed immediately due to their tendency to break and to increase the tree's vigor and size, due to the strong growth signal they send the tree, which delays early fruiting (or precocity, on which this method depends).

The spindle technique uses bending or branch manipulation more than pruning to achieve its weeping fruitful form. You can use rubber bands, wires (as with bonsai trees), clothespins, and bamboo stakes with ties.

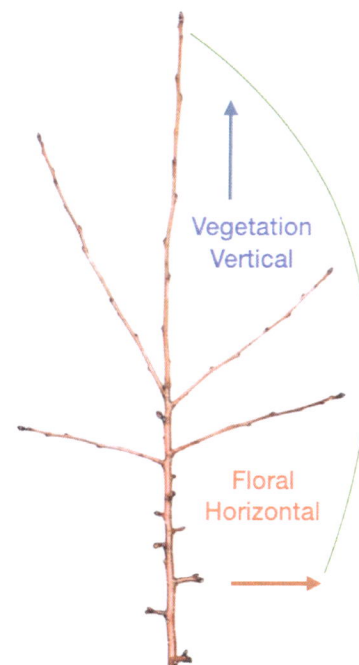

Vegetation
Vertical

Floral
Horizontal

Side Shoot 5

Tree Pricing and Grading
Why Nursery Tree Size Matters

The best tree to start with is the grade 0 or 1 on a dwarfing rootstock. **(See the next chapter for more details on rootstocks.)** The best dwarf trees are found by nurseries that supply trees for the wholesale spindle-tree market but also sell smaller retail orders. If you start with a small tree, you are likely going to need an extra year or two to achieve the early fruit-bearing results that commercial growers get wholesale in large bundles of grade 0

	2-YEAR TREES			1-YEAR TREES	
"Fancy" Grade 0	Grade 1	Grade 2	Grade 3	Grade 4	Grade 5
1-19 $42.00	1-19 $38.25	1-19 $37.25	1-19 $36.25	1-19 $26.75	1-19 $21.25
20-49 $42.00	20-49 $34.25	20-49 $33.25	20-49 $32.25	20-49 $24.75	20-49 $18.25
50-99 $42.00	50-99 $29.75	50-99 $28.75	50-99 $27.75	50-99 $21.25	50-99 $15.75
100-499 $42.00	100-499 $24.75	100-499 $23.75	100-499 $22.75	100-499 $16.25	100-499 $12.75

to 1 trees. See the table for a 2023 sample from Cummins Nursery.

You pay a premium to buy a larger, older tree; but with those trees, nurseries will have grown the rootstock for one year before grafting, so you get a good strong start. Royalties for patented varieties are not included in the chart.

Typical Nursery Tree Grade Spectrum

Grades 5-4	Grades 3-2	Grades 2-1	Grade 0
1-year-old shoot	2-year-old shoot	2-year-old shoot	2-year-old shoot
1-year-old root	2-year-old root	2-year-old root	2-year-old root
18-36 inches tall	32-42 inches tall	42-54 inches tall	50-72 inches tall
1/4-inch caliper (diameter)	3/8-inch caliper	1/2-inch caliper	3/4-inch caliper
No laterals or flower spurs	Few laterals/spurs	Few more laterals/spurs	More than 3-5 laterals/spurs
Half the cost of Grade 0			Twice the cost of Grade 5

Gradation varies with rootstocks and varieties. Grades 0 through 3 can give you a three-year head start; if you raise your own trees, you could take four years to get to the 3/4-inch caliper. Some wholesale suppliers have Grade 0 with more than 12 laterals

Training Goals for Years 0 to 5

Year 0: Planning the Autumn and Spring Planting

Planning

The year before planting Year 0, decide which varieties and rootstock, location, supports, supplies, labels, and any plant protection you'll use. Shop around and get your orders in early before supplies get limited.

Storage

You may need to store your trees until ready for planting. Follow instruction from nursery. I keep mine in a bucket with damp potting mix in the unheated garage or on a North facing shady wall.

Support

Install individual stakes at time of planting. Remember to order enough ahead of time

Planting

Timing: Before leafing out ~March to May Depending on your climate zone you might be able to plant in Autumn.

Method: Dig a hole that can accommodate the roots. Leave graft union three inches above soil level (see the next chapter, on rootstocks). If the roots seem dry, you can soak them in cold water for 30 to 120 minutes. Bare-root trees often don't have a lot of roots. Spread them out and trim any damaged roots. It's important to firm the soil well to make good soil-to-root contact

Trio Planting: Plant trees two to four feet apart in a triangle. Each tree gets an upright stake (I like Takiron,* 5/8-inch × 8-foot, with 18 to 24 inches in-ground). Some growers just use metal posts. Use 7/16- to 1/2-inch bamboo with vinyl tape to create a triangular tower. **Prepare for branch manipulation during the first growing season by** bending down thicker laterals with heavy rubber bands, wire, or bamboo stakes with ties; remove these in late summer.

* Takiron is available at Gardener's Edge or A. M. Leonard.

Year 1: First Leaf and Summer Training Goals

The first-year goals are as follows:

- Attach the **leader** to its support as it grows toward the top.

- Remove any codominate leaders before growth starts, roughly in **March.**

- Bend down **laterals** from the previous year's growth before they leaf out.

- Direct **new laterals** down and out in **May through July.**

Clothes pin to lower lateral shoot

Where's the Top? How High?

Commercial growers use a variation called the tall spindle, growing plants to 10 feet or taller, simply to promote the greatest efficiency of space. These are often planted in long rows only 10 feet apart and hundreds of feet long. Small-scale growers have more flexibility because your spacing is not about machinery. I suggest aiming for supports that are around six feet tall, where the leader will be bent back down after it reaches seven or eight feet. (See the next chapter, on rootstocks.)

Notching in May/June

If you have empty gaps along the trunk of your new tree, you can encourage more laterals to grow using the notching technique in May and June. See Side Shoot 6. I plan on getting video clips up on my YouTube channel at The Social Gardener.

Thinning

Contrary to conventional trees, which sometimes delay fruiting because they are building scaffolding branches, with the spindle method *some* early fruiting can be allowed, especially if you start with high-quality Grade 0 or 1 trees. In Year 1 this can lead to five fruits or fewer. Your main goal is to set flowers on laterals for the next year.

Summer Branch Manipulation

During the first year you'll need a stake to train the central leader straight up. You can use wires, bamboo skewers, and even clothespins to bend lateral shoots down during that critical window between July and August so that the tree will set flower buds for the coming year.

Floral tape and floral wire are available at craft stores. Floral tape can be applied to clothespins to act as weights to bend branches or can be used in combination with floral wire and/or skewers to create longer flexible trainers to attach to laterals. In this way you anticipate summer growth with the ability to bend branches as they grow— like how bonsai wire manipulates branches to create shapes.

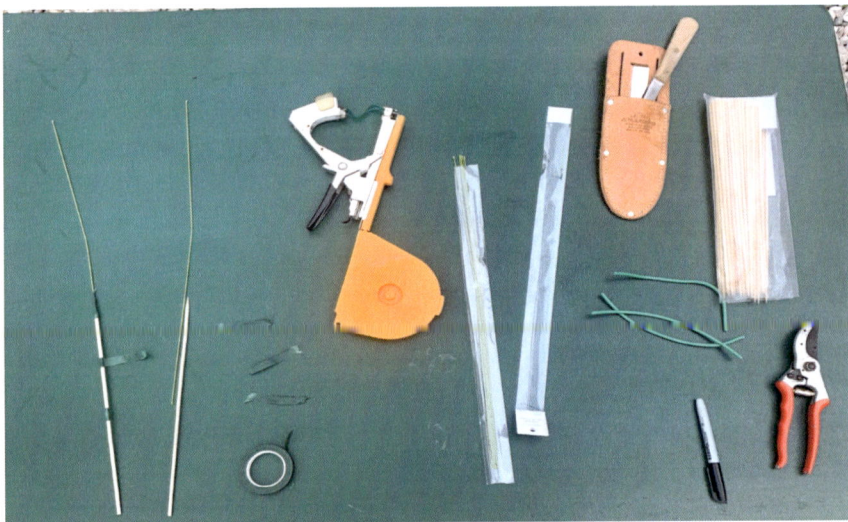

The point is that once you've identified a branch as a future fruiting lateral, make sure to bend it down during the summer to switch the plant's growth energy from vegetative to floral (and thus to fruit).

Some of My Favorite Tools

I've used the Max Tapener, a tying tool from A. M. Leonard, for more than 30 years. It works like a tying tool and stapler combined. It allows you to attach a wrap around a branch and a bamboo stake using one hand to operate the tool and the other to bring the branch into position. I use it to tie cucumbers, tomatoes, sweet peas, grapevines, bramble canes, espalier branches, and spindle tree laterals.

For main branches I'll use bamboo, cut using a hacksaw (bamboo splinters easily). For smaller branches I'll use skewers and various types and gauges of wire.

For fastening I'll use florist tape for light temporary attachments or reusable Velcro strips, sold at garden centers, for longer-term needs.

Clothespins are also very adaptable and reusable ways to weight branches as well as attaching them to supports. You can wrap the clothespin jaws with floral tape if you need a stickier attachment. Again, the goal here is to bend lateral branches down during the summer to encourage next year's flower buds to set, while allowing just one upright leader.

Side Shoot 6

Notching

Notching is a technique used on young trees to stimulate spurs and laterals to grow and fill in blank spots along the trunk.

These pictures show how you can cut a crescent shape above a dormant bud to encourage the tree to break dormancy and initiate a flower spur to form during the growing season.

It doesn't always lead to a full-blown lateral shoot but can help fill in a gap. It temporarily disrupts the descending hormone from the uppermost leader, which otherwise suppresses subordinate buds and branches; this disruption helps release the sleeping bud directly below the cut. It all begins with an apically dominant lead shoot, or leader.

Notching is an old espalier technique. **Notching works best during the first half of summer, when vegetative growth is most active.**

Initial Notch May 7

Same notch 5 weeks later—June 15

Year 2: Second Leaf Training Goals

The second summer after planting, your goals include the following:

- Establishing dominance of the leader in forming the central spindle in caliper and height
- Establishing wide-angled laterals starting 12 to 24 inches from ground level

Dormant Season

The **dormant season** is just before leafing out. It varies according to zones: March in Zone 7, April in Zone 6, May in Zones 5 to 4, etc.

- If the **leader** has not grown above the top of its stake, leave it unpruned.

- If the **leader** has grown past the top of its stake, bend it over, using a heavy rubber band or training wire like it's another a lateral branch.

Summer Training

- Don't prune any replacement leaders that may shoot from the top. Wait and bend them down in late June to early July.

- Keep **laterals** from previous year's growth bent down below the horizontal. Aim to have five or more 18- to 24-inch **laterals.**

- If you have blank spots along the central leader (or spindle), use the notching technique (see Side Shoot 6) to encourage more **laterals or spurs to grow.**

- Thin the fruits in June, leaving fewer than 15 fruits strategically placed to help further bend the **laterals.**

- In late June, pinch back the tips of any **laterals** getting **too** long (more than 28 inches) by about three inches.

Year 3: Training Goals

The third summer after planting, your goals include the following.

Dormant Season

- Do not cut back the leader. Rather, bend it down if it is too tall.

- If any limbs are overly vigorous—for example, codominant limbs greater than 60% of the leader's diameter—cut them back using the bevel cut (see Side Shoot 7).

Summer Training

- In June, thin excess fruit, leaving fewer than 50 fruits per tree—a little more if the tree is growing strongly, and a little fewer if growing weakly.

- In July, check if the main leader needs tying down.

- In July, make sure all laterals are bent down.

- In late July, pinch back any laterals that are too long (longer than 28 inches).

Year 4: Training Goals

The fourth summer after planting your goals include the following.

Dormant Season

- Do not cut back the leader. Rather, bend it down if it is too tall.

- If any limbs are overly vigorous—for example, codominant limbs greater than 60% of the leader's diameter—cut them back using the bevel cut (see Side Shoot 7).

Summer Training

- In June, thin excess fruit, leaving fewer than 50 fruits per tree—a little more if tree is growing strongly—fewer if growing weakly.

- In July, check if the main Leader needs tying down.

- In July, make sure all laterals are bent down.

> Thinning apples is the removal of excess fruits leaving about one apple every 4-6" of branch. Or about one fruit per 25 leaves to maintain a a healthy 'economy' between vegetation and fruit.
>
> Optimum Cropping Targets per Healthy Spindle tree by year –
> Year 1   1-5 fruits
> Year 2   15 fruits
> Year 3   40 fruits
> Year 4   70 fruits
> Year 5   90 fruits
>
> Results vary according to climate, vigor and health of trees

Side Shoot 7

The Bevel Cut

The bevel cut is a technique unique to the spindle method that breaks the normal pruning rule of not leaving a stub. It has a specific reason and desired outcome.

In the diagram here,

- **A** is the central spindle or trunk.
- **B** is an older lateral, more than 60% the diameter of **A,** needing renewal using the bevel cut.
- **C** is the bevel cut, leaving a bud on the underside to replace the older, larger lateral. In its second through sixth years it will be fruitful.

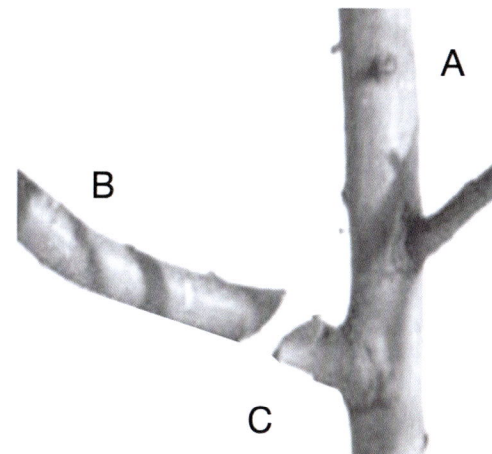

Big branches lead to big trees. The goal in the spindle method is one central trunk eventually covered with 20 or so heavily fruiting laterals. After the central trunk is well established, your focus shifts to renewing laterals. Yet this renewal must not overstimulate vegetative growth along with weak weeping laterals.

The bevel cut achieves this end by pointing the growth into a downward-facing bud. The bevel cut stimulates a replacement lateral that already is inclined to the horizontal position of a fruiting lateral. Together with the influence of the dwarfing rootstock, these new laterals start flowering and fruiting as early as the following year.

The maintenance pruning of the spindle during years 5 through 20 involves removing one or two of the oldest biggest laterals, often in the middle region of the spindle. (Arborists call this a "subordination" of the laterals to the central leader, keeping the overall tree small yet new and healthy.)

A gardener might think of how canes on a bramble fruit or an elderberry bush are renewed to the base—only in this case, the laterals are renewed to the trunk of the woody tree rather than to ground level. We might call these laterals "canes" that are replaced after around six years.

The bevel cut thus works with the biology of pome fruits, especially apples, on dwarfing rootstocks.

Wow—so simple compared to pruning a large standard tree with all its secondary scaffold branches!

Years 5 to 20: Mature Tree Maintenance

Dormant Season

•Limit tree height by cutting the leader back to a fruitful side branch.

•Use the bevel cut technique to remove up to three laterals larger than 60% of the diameter of the trunk, especially those found in the middle or upper region of the trunk.

Actual mature height will vary depending on conditions especially rootstock choice

Summer Training

•In June, thin excess fruit, leaving 100 to 120 fruits per tree—a little more if the tree is growing strongly, and a little fewer if growing weakly.

•In August, prune laterals to allow good air flow and light penetration. This means thinning or reducing laterals, but don't overdo it.

By this point you've grown as an apple gardener and can reassess your rootstock and variety choices. Cornell University recommends replanting around 5% of your trees annually so that your experience and knowledge helps your garden keep moving in the best direction.

How Pome Fruits Are Different . . .

When you eat an apple and discard the core, you're eating not the fruit but a modified stem.

Botanists describe the special form of a pome fruit as having an "inferior ovary," because in taxonomy plants are categorized by the number and arrangement of their flower parts. In pome fruits—like a pear, apple, or Quince—the ovary is retracted below the other flower parts (sepals, petals, and stamens) and consists of five carpels containing seeds in a single compound ovary. This arrangement is called "inferior," meaning "below" in scientific terms, rather than implying judgment. The term acknowledges an evolutionary adaptation.

Two Reasons Why This Biology Is Important

The first reason has to do with the energy dynamic: more fruits mean fewer shoots. And vice versa: overpruning leads to more shoots and fewer fruits. Overpruning is a common mistake.

Judicious pruning takes energy that would have gone into wood or shoot production and redirects into creating a sweet "woody fruit" instead. Apples' superpower as a woody fruit is that they store well, often for months, rather than just days as with other fruits. Some varieties get better in storage.

Historically, this storage capacity has been valuable to folks in the northern hemisphere with shorter growing seasons. When apple growing became more commercialized, regional varieties with lower storability couldn't compete with mass production, storage, and shipping of more storable apples from places like Washington state.

For homesteaders and other regional growers, however, the apple's ability to store and travel well makes for a potential renaissance for regional niche varieties that can boost local foodie culture with a low carbon footprint.

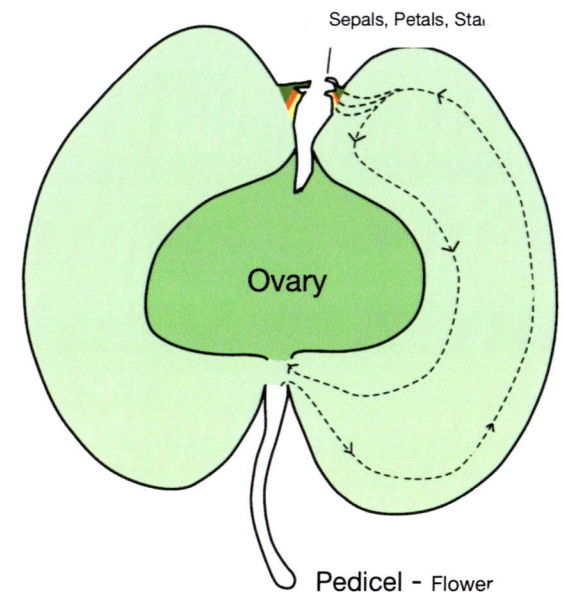

Sepals, Petals, Sta

Ovary

Pedicel - Flower

Image –Wikimedia Commons, Public Domain

ROOTSTOCKS

The Two-Part Tree: Rootstock and Variety

When you buy an apple tree, you are actually making a double purchase: (1) the named **variety,** which usually catches your interest first, is the tree's top, and (2) the **rootstock** on which it is grafted is the tree's base and root.

If the nursery label doesn't identify the exact rootstock type, you might not be shopping in the right place because the choice of rootstock is as critical to success as the variety is. You can always change the variety later by top-working, or grafting additional varieties on top, but you can't change the rootstock later.

If you look at the base of most fruit trees, you'll see a swelling known as the "**graft union.**" Below is the rootstock, and above is the named fruiting variety, also known as the "scion." The next chapter goes into grafting, but for now every consumer should know they are purchasing a two-part tree and what those parts are specifically.

You may see other shoots rising from below the graft union; these are suckers springing up and are daughters of the rootstock, as shown in the photo example. Some rootstock varieties sucker more than others. Yes, they can be a nuisance, and cutting them out often makes the problem worse. As early in spring as possible, on a wet day, try to pluck them out of their attachments to the root—much like rubbing out an unwanted shoot on a branch while it's still young, without having to cut it. You might have to dig around a bit. You can also select rootstocks that sucker less.

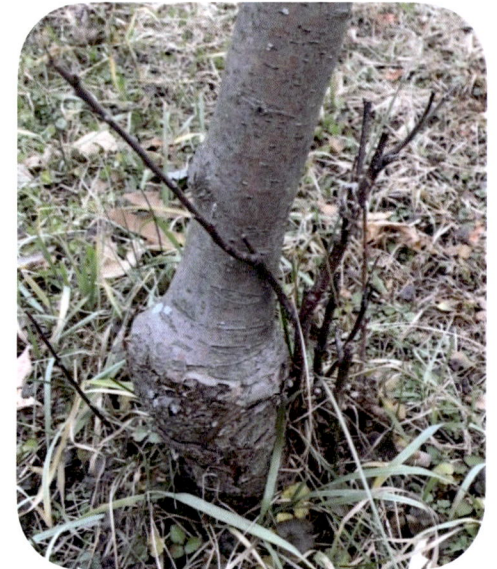

Why Are Most Fruit Trees Grafted?

Although fruit trees could be grown as cuttings, grafting onto known **rootstock "clones"** (rootstocks that are themselves grown from cuttings) using selected rootstocks can overcome certain diseases, influence mature size, improve lateral branch angle attachments, and induce early fruiting, known as "**precocity.**" When you know about different rootstock options, you can plan better for size, spacing, and growing system. This is **essential** to the spindle method.

Selecting the right rootstock is **both an art and a science** that is still being field-tested by commercial growers, who tend to choose smaller rootstocks in wetter climates and larger ones in more arid climates. Many hobby growers who are not familiar with the spindle method go in search of the elusive free-standing yet early-fruiting sweet spot among rootstocks. These qualities seem to be somewhat mutually exclusive, so you must plan accordingly—wait longer for fruit while the spindle structure is established, or provide support during the establishment phase with a smaller rootstock.

A Wide Range of Apple Rootstock Choices and Sizes

Standard	100% height	Over 30 feet tall
Semi-Dwarf	40-60% height	12 to 18 feet tall
Dwarf	10-40% height	3 to 12 feet tall

Growers give percentages because rootstock performance varies by region and rainfall. **Standard** trees may be used in harsh environments under pressure from grazing animals. But shadow and accessibility factors are challenging. **Semi-dwarfs** can be self-supporting and are used in cider and apple-processing orchards. Dwarf rootstocks are what you want for Spindle trees.

Standard or Seedling Size

Semi-Dwarf Size

Dwarf

Side Shoot 9

Difference Between a Bush and a Tree

Hint: It's not size . . . it's where new growth occurs—at the *top or base*.

Most trees initiate new growth at the top. This pattern is especially true of trees with apical dominance (see "Apples 101" at the beginning of this book). But unlike trees, bushes—like lilacs, forsythia, or roses—eventually need to replace canes, stems, or branches from their base. They don't have a tree's vascular structures to sustain a permanent trunk that initiates new growth from the top down.

This means bushes are pruned differently from trees. Bushes are often pruned harder in order to stimulate new branches that bear flowers and fruits. Trees, especially conifers, initiate new growth from the top every year—so much so that their size increases annually but their roughly conical form remains the same for many years until they lose that form in response to their environment, including other trees and buildings.

Apple trees tend to grow upright throughout their establishment and middle years before gradually becoming more rounded and umbrella shaped. On standard or seedling rootstock apple trees, this process can take 45 to 60 years, in three phases requiring up to 15 years for each phase.

The spindle method **doesn't reduce the tree form to a bush entirely**—that would require renewal by pruning back to the base. Rather, to maintain the mature spindle, fruiting canes or **laterals need renewal pruning along the trunk** or spindle at the rate of about two winter bevel cuts each dormant season. This effort saves commercial growers with who plant more than 20,000 trees per acre.

This time savings also extends to you, the apple gardener. Yet it requires a mind shift from the older orchard systems that required a lot of winter pruning using ladders among tall trees.

The resulting culture of using special rootstocks and training techniques makes for a spindle form that is neither tree (initiating top growth) nor a bush (requiring renewal from the base), but is rather something of a partnership between you and your tree. It is akin to how bonsai practice creates a miniature version of an older tree.

In the Side Shoot 8, I showed how this method relies on and works with the unique biology of pome fruits. Plants have a limited energy budget to spend on their growth, maintenance, and reproduction. Their "energy income" comes primarily from photosynthesis, with some added from biological and chemical soil partnerships. Helping your trees regulate this income and expense balancing between vegetative renewal and fruit yield is how you maintain the health and longevity of your spindle trees.

Rootstock Naming and Numbers

Apples have perhaps the greatest number of rootstock choices available of any fruit. Research stations around the world use a letter abbreviation and a number to identify different rootstock clones. In the 1880s, the Apple Research Station in Kent in the United Kingdom began identifying dwarfing rootstocks that were smaller and well-suited for espalier and other high-density planting systems. These are the **MM** series, referring to Malling/Merton. **P** refers to Polish rootstocks, **B** to Budagosvky (from Russia), and **G** to the rootstock series from Geneva, New York.

Here I'll mention a few standard and semi-dwarf rootstocks, but this book focuses on the dwarf selections suitable for spindle-type trees.

- **Standard**: MM.111, B.118, P.18, and various seedling strains
- **Semi-Dwarf**: G.202, G.210, G.935, G.969, G.890, M.7, MM.111
- **Dwarf**: B.9, M.9, G.11, G.16, G.214, G.41

These specific dwarfing rootstocks are the preferred rootstocks for spindle trees in most climates, especially those with more than 25 inches of annual rain, with permanent plant support. Most commercial growers that use the spindle method are favoring the smaller rootstocks, especially **G.11** and **G.41**.

New rootstocks are coming into use on a regular basis as the research for the perfect rootstock continues.

These specialty rootstocks are available in bundles of 500 to 1,000 trees for commercial growers who plant more than 1,000 trees per acre in high-density settings using variations on the spindle method. Growers get high-quality trees that are already two years old at planting.

The trees pictured on the right are in their second leaf and are bearing their first fruits on M.9 rootstocks. With 20,000 trees on 20 acres, this grower had limited time to bend down branches as much as recommended, while fruiting early helps divert some of the vigor from the top. For years, M.9 was a favorite of commercial growers due to its precocity and small size. Yet in areas with more than 30 inches of annual precipitation, the M.9 rootstock plants often become too large to handle. So many growers are shifting to G.41 or G.11. Here in arid Colorado in the Front Range, I'm leaning toward G.969 and even G.890. It's a constant learning process, however, and that's part of the journey.

Search for the Perfect Rootstock

In a perfect world, you could have a rootstock that is more vigorous while the spindle tree is young and getting established and then becomes more precocious after the tree is established—but you have to pick one. For the spindle tree, you have to provide support. The search for the perfect rootstock is a very site-specific choice that is only confirmed when the tree reaches maturity in 6 to 20 years. The result of the rootstock and variety combination is a complex mix of factors including variety, rootstock, training, rainfall, soil health and fertility, and climate—all leading to the ultimate mature spindle-tree size and productivity. Each factors adds or subtracts from the result.

This mix of factors makes it hard to create a one-size-fits-all rootstock. That said, I have observed a big regional difference between rootstock performance east and west of the Mississippi: an ecological divide between the more humid Eastern deciduous woodlands environment and the more arid Western prairie, which transitions from tall to short grasslands to a desert environment. Soil types that occur in those corresponding regions also influence the performance of spindle trees.

General Rootstock Suggestions

- Western US (Less Than 35 Inches of Annual Precipitation): G.202, G. 890, G.969, B.118, MM.111, and P.18.
- Eastern US (More Than 35 Inches of Annual Precipitation): G.11, G.30, G.41, G.935.

While living in Pennsylvania for years, I tried to find a self-supporting rootstock that also had the precocity of the smaller trees that make the spindle method so space-efficient and accessible. I since have learned that you should plan on providing continuous support for the spindle technique. Commercial growers make a big investment in the trellis system, which I've found useful when using large equipment such as tractors, trailers, sprayers, etc. But gardeners who work on a smaller scale in more diverse landscapes can plant using trio support structures to save money and avoid large monoculture plantations.

As previously mentioned, install stakes at the same time as planting to avoid damage during installation. You can use *T*-posts that are 8 to 10 feet tall from a hardware store or purchase vinyl-coated posts from Gardener's Supply and other suppliers.

HOME GRAFTING

Home Grafting

At some point you might want to try your hand at grafting. In this technique, you create another tree by taking a cutting from an existing variety that you like and, rather than rooting it in the soil, you "root" or graft it onto a specific rootstock type.

This form of vegetative propagation brings together two known elements with predictable outcomes. With practice and planning, *timing, temperature, tools,* and *techniques* come together with delightful results that you can share with others.

The example on the far right shows a graft made on April 25 one year that grew to over three feet tall by August 1. The variety was Honeycrisp, the rootstock was Geneva 969, and the container was a three-gallon fabric pot. The soil was a mix of a soil-moisture control blend plus around 10% perlite for added drainage.

All of these details can be varied to fit your situation. The following year, I switched to smaller tree pots (about 4 x 9 inches) to save space and to make it easier to move the initial grafts indoors during the first few weeks while the union heals. Here in Colorado's Zone 5, variable springtime weather fluctuations can delay the formation of a good union.

The arrow alongside the growth photo shows how every branch is a calendar solidified in space, with each leaf, bud, and branch node having a birthdate spanning April to August. By learning to read these seasonal growth patterns, you can get a sense of the health and history of a mature tree in the landscape. This is what a nursery does one or two years before it sells a tree.

8/1
7/26
7/18
7/11
7/4
6/27
6/20
6/13
6/5
5/30
5/23
5/16
5/9
5/2
4/25

Timeline of a one-year-old grafted apple tree

What You Need and How It Works

Because tools, timing, and technique are key to success, you'll want to have these supplies at the ready.

Scions: In January, gather 6-inch pencil-width scions from the varieties you want, and store them in labeled ziplock bags in the refrigerator **until you are ready to graft in April or May.** Alternately, **order scions by mail in December through January** and store them until ready.

Rootstocks: After you've researched the rootstocks you want, you can mail-order these too. Most places run out, so you want to get your order in as early as possible, at least by **December**.

Containers and Soil Media: Order the containers and have enough soil media to fill the containers you plan on using.

Tools and Supplies: Sharp, clean hand clippers; grafting knife; grafting tape or buddy tape; vinyl electricians' tape; plant labels; a permanent marker; and bamboo skewers.

How It Works

I think of grafting as "rooting a cutting" in the stem of a parent tree rather than directly in the soil. **Time this for just** before the rootstock starts growing. A short piece of scion, about two inches long with two buds, is united on top of the rootstock using matching cut surfaces. A piece of grafting tape seals this union, and a tight wrap of vinyl tape holds it in place without contacting the bark. See the demonstration video at the QR code in this section.

As you'll see in the linked video, there are many different types of grafts, such as the whip and tongue, but I like the **cleft graft** because it holds two parts together while I get ready to wrap the union. Unions have a nasty habit of breaking, so I attach a bamboo skewer to act as a splint.

Having everything ready at hand means you can do this in a minute or two. Around two weeks ahead of time, I plant the rootstocks in pots and write the label with the scion variety and the rootstock type, attaching the label around the base of the little tree. That step is important because you are joining a region just below the bark, called the cambium, where growth and cellular division occurs. It's just a few cells thick and *can't dry out—or move afterwards*. This key phase is why I double-tape—first with the grafting tape, which is waxy and stretchy, to make a seal; and then with the second tape, common electrical tape, for strength so that the union does not move at all. The tape can be removed in September. Tightness won't hurt the growing tree.

https://
youtu.be/
Snm15DqQ
MwU

Cleft Grafting
Video

Note that large-scale growers do this differently, using a technique called bench grafting that skips potting. The grafted trees go directly into temporary beds with a simple soil-free media. Later they are planted in field rows to grow for a year before being graded and sorted for sale during the bare-root shipping season.

A Closer Look at Basic Grafting Tools

The main tools are a good pair of hand clippers (I like Felco 2) and a grafting knife that is as sharp as a scalpel. If anything can be called "tree surgery," it's grafting. I've used the same grafting knife for more than 30 years. I personally prefer the fixed-blade type over the various pocket-folding types, although good versions of those can be used in budding, which is often done in August—but I'm not describing that technique here.

In the photo on the left, I'm using a three-gallon fabric pot. I've since switched to a 4x4x9-inch tree pot, shown on the next page, which I later pot up to a two-gallon air pot between eight and ten weeks later. Plants from air pots are easier to transplant than those from the fabric pots, which tend to suck up the most delicate fibrous roots; these then get damaged during transplanting.

I use a small 1x30-inch belt sander with special-ordered fine-grit belts (600 to 100 grit) from Amazon to keep my tools sharp. I also use coarser belts, which are more readily available, for touching up garden tools.

I keep my grafting knife in a sheath holder (shown on page 33) because it is so scary-sharp. I'm working on putting links on my website, including videos. Coming soon is a video on practicing cleft grafting, as you shouldn't try to do the actual grafting without practicing your knife and wrapping skills first, using practice materials like willow or poplar whips. I'll get more videos up as I get around to it and hear more questions that you may have.

Post-Grafting Care and Top-Working

In regions cooler than USDA Zone 9, you should also think about post-grafting care. This stage is where small tree containers come in handy. During the first 12 to 36 hours, the union between the rootstock and scion will take place—or not. Based on my experience, the process works best with damp but not soggy soil at a temperature between 45 and 55°F. Some folks use more heat, but I don't like to push it too much.

I'm in Zone 5, where we can have some real cold dry spells in late spring. So I'll bring the pots indoors for the first few days before moving them to an unheated garage and then outdoors. I also tent the newly grafted trees to prevent drying out (as shown in the photo with the trash bags).

You might not need to do all that, but it helps, with a success rate of 90% or higher. Shoots can take three to four weeks to arise from both the scion and the rootstock. I usually wait a little before rubbing out the shoots from the rootstock (that is, any buds below the black vinyl tape), and then I leave only one from the scion as the dominant leader. Or you might leave two shoots if you plan to cut one out the following January to graft more of that variety.

Look for Top-working fruit trees

Top-working is when you graft not onto a new rootstock but onto an existing tree. This is how "Frankenstein" trees are created with many varieties grafted onto a single tree. Keeping track of labels is always a challenge. In addition to labeling, take lots of pictures so that when you lose a label you have something to refer to. Rather than creating multigrafted trees, however, I prefer to cultivate a collection of small trees instead. If you are top-working, just remember how an upright position creates strong vegetative growth, good for changing a tree over to a new variety, versus a more horizontal position that can give you a small fruiting lateral so you can taste and test a new variety that you might want to grow more of in the future.

Un-wrapped top graft in progress ⟶

Why It Matters

Side Shoot #10

Primary Purpose of Gardening

There really is no one-size-fits-all recipe for gardening. Still, we get a lot of inspiration from seeing what others are doing, including their failures and successes. Even if we don't live and learn on a multigenerational farm, the nature of our craft has deep roots in the countless generations of farmers and gardeners—roots that are steeped in reverence, gratitude, and honor. Something greater than ourselves is growing us, and we have a responsibility to pass this living legacy on to the next generation.

Ancient and traditional peoples saw nature more clearly with their heart and hands, not just their head, such that they might say: "Within the life and legacy of these domesticated crops and livestock are contained all the food we shall ever need, so long as we care, tend, and preserve them." This understanding goes back to the origin of agriculture, when humans still experienced food as a gift of living nature that continually shed its life for us while overcoming the forces of decay and death.

I was reminded of this in the Dominican Republic as part of a rural developmental program to replace slash-and-burn practices with more sustainable ones. Epiphanio replied to the question: What is agriculture? and said Honor. Traditional cultures remember truths and techniques that we have forgotten yet are gradually rediscovering in ways that meet this moment of climate crisis. You will find your own reasons why gardening matters. You may surprise yourself. I can confidently say that gardening feeds me: body, soul, and spirit. And that I need that sustenance on all those levels every day.

One of my most satisfying accomplishments as a gardening teacher at a K-12 school was when my ninth- and tenth-grade students could assist and lead my third-grade students in activities that they themselves had done years earlier. The school garden is cultivated more **for** the younger child and **by** the older students. This philosophy is how I attempted to create a miniature multigenerational experience within a school garden program. Thirty years later, we had a reunion that brought those students back with children of their own, and we experienced how this works over a longer time span, even over generations.

To practice farming and gardening is to cultivate honor in all that has come before and all that will come after us.

1. Hope Is Fueled by Results

I'm confident that apple gardening using the spindle method will become a cherished part of your gardening journey. In this section and those that follow, I offer examples of why this journey matters to me. More important to me is hearing about your experiences, about what fuels your gardening passion. People take up gardening for many reasons: your pocketbook, your emotional and physical health, your family, your neighborhood, the environment, social justice, the planet, even peace, or just the sheer joy and surprise of gardening.

Lately we seem to be recognizing that things in the world are not as we would like them to be: whether those include the world's kindness, safety, community, joy, hope, health, security—the list goes on. No doubt you can add more. For me gardening has always been about restoring all these things while daring to dream that best is yet to come—for me, for you, for everyone, for this amazing planet. It's worth caring for; it's worth hoping for. As a gardening teacher for many years, I love seeing how a garden grows so many good things, especially our ability to be more caring, generous, and responsible people through formative experiences in the garden. All of these experiences contain a wealth of antidotes to the many forces that threaten to defeat, depress, deflate, and drag us down.

I hate to see anyone get discouraged or grow cynical, especially gardeners! We can change the world, even if just one little place and moment at a time. In doing so we also change ourselves and exercise our rights to life, liberty, and the pursuit of happiness. May your gardening journey strengthen your enthusiasm to pursue your deepest dreams and hopes.

I'm excited that every gardener can learn what the spindle method can do for you and your garden, whether you're an old pro or a beginner. In a few years, you could be growing six months' worth of quality apples in less space than you imagined possible. When you know firsthand how easy it is, you'll want to add more to your cropping program—and you'll know exactly how to do it. Start with quality and adjust the quantity as you need. As David Mallett sings, "Inch by inch, row by row."

Along the way you'll discover that a virtuous cycle of giving, forgiving, and generosity has been bestowed upon your garden, and you will delight in sharing your experience with others in a way that satisfies you like few other creative activities do. Hope that is fulfilled with results can restore faith and confidence—in ourselves and our resiliency to overcome setbacks.

The spindle technique has reinvigorated commercial systems and can similarly offer hope and inspiration for small-scale gardeners. It bugs me to no end to see gardeners giving up on apples because they are stuck in a standard orchard model of big old trees with big old problems. Everything about the spindle method is more accessible, more productive, and easier to manage. Just as every gardener knows how homegrown fruits like tomatoes and strawberries far surpass anything that's available in supermarkets—so too you will rediscover the wholesome goodness in apples that has largely been forgotten. Every victory garden needs a few spindle trees!

2. Multifunctional Landscapes Foster Virtuous Cycles of Health, Quality, and Sustainability

More folks are expanding their notion of what a landscape is intended for, does, and provides. Even though new housing developments always put in a lawn with a few trees and bushes, these are often just window dressing for sales and curb appeal. Often, in addition to the hasty plant selections, the soil underneath has been damaged by grading and site preparation for building. The new resident wonders why things are growing poorly.

New trends are emerging that might be called multifunctional landscapes, in which a more holistic approach to ecological health integrates a multitude of landscape features and functions. Pollinator plants or edibles are examples of a multifunctional landscape. You still need all your hardscaping bones with paths, fencing, patios, irrigation, raised beds, structures, and so on . . . but you need living factors (shall we say "softscaping" in contrast to hardscaping?) that will improve with care over time and whose combined orchestration will mature in ways that hardscaping can't. Such softscaping can imitate natural landscapes where slope, exposure, soil, ground covers, shrubs, and trees blend in space and season to mutually support one another. All great gardens do this in unique regional ways. Designers often begin with hardscaping, while the ongoing care provided by gardeners comes to life via the softscaping.

Ecological gardeners always tend to balance these hard and soft aspects in the multifunctional landscape so that a kind of symbiosis brings out a site-specific quality contrasted with mere quantity. On the other hand, we are likely to see production-focused agriculture swing to as much of a hardscape-controlled environment as possible. We already see this with intensive indoor animal feed lots and sprawling apple plantations using the spindle method. Such vast monocultural operations tend to require high energy, feed, fertilizer, and chemical inputs.

But your patio, backyard, community, or school garden design doesn't have to go that way.

Instead, you can adapt the best aspects from modern production systems that fit your situation. For example, a dozen spindle trees can do wonders in your garden as a middle canopy layer rather than an upper canopy. But a thousand trees per acre may push you in a direction you're not really seeking. A multifunctional landscape gives you the freedom to mix and match the elements that best meet your evolving interests and needs in your landscape. Let form and function mesh with your lifestyle and goals.

In your multifunctional landscape, you will come to discover how elements you may have overlooked before can become your best friends. These may include native plants, beneficial insects, birds, composting, season extension and protection techniques, vertical gardening, plant propagation, outdoor living spaces, water features, garden clubs, cooking and food preservation, and much more.

3. Every Garden Can Demonstrate Ecoliteracy and Sustainable Stewardship in Action

It's one thing to say that how we care for the planet informs the overall health of humanity. It's another thing to show it in practice, even in just a small school or community garden. In my first book, I described creating a school garden program to fill an agro-eco gap in education so that the next generation can have practical insight into future decisions. This approach goes together with the "know what's right—do what's possible" approach to avoid burnout. Your interest and passion will guide you in finding which aspect of ecoliteracy your garden will demonstrate and make visible to your community.

Gardening can demonstrate many practices:

- Sequester carbon by removing atmospheric CO_2 into biomass, a process that woody perennials do particularly well.
- Enhance habitats for wildlife that help sustain local ecosystems.
- Reduce the carbon footprint associated with food travel, packaging, display, and energy consumption costs in the supply chain.
- Provide fresh, nutrient-dense foods.
- Educate the public about stewardship, environment, and quality.
- Promote pride in local produce and agricultural careers.
- Foster multigenerational interactions at community and senior centers.
- Provide service opportunities at school gardens.
- Promote water and soil conservation.
- Foster economic and aesthetic development.
- Make possible nature-based therapy opportunities.
- Offer court-adjudicated service opportunities.
- Learn from Native elders.
- Put on festivals and build community.

Side Shoot 11

What Makes Something an Heirloom?

An heirloom is passed down from one generation to another.

So is the "heirloom" label a matter of time? Is an object an heirloom if it is older than 25 years? There are no hard and fast rules—yet in addition to the passage of time, other values contribute to the heirloom status of something. For example: "This was my grandmother's ring . . . I remember it on her hand." Yet memories can get lost over the generations.

But when that heirloom is not an object but a living organism, it lives on as part of the living DNA of that organism. Since the Industrial Revolution and especially over the past 50 years, fewer domesticated plants and animals fit well into modern industrialized systems, with all their machinery and uniformity. Heirlooms and biodiversity tend to get lost.

There are seed banks and living collections that attempt to preserve as great a collection as possible, recognizing that the finality of lost species and varieties reduces our resilience in adapting to changing environments.

Saving seeds and preserving regionally adapted varieties can be a win-win for small-scale gardens. Local, regional, national, and international organizations are eager to expand their partnerships and are willing to share both seeds and knowledge. Start with one heirloom plant . . . and see how it goes.

As mentioned earlier, thousands of apple varieties exist. Just because some have fallen out of commercial favor, that doesn't mean they don't have value or virtue. It just takes a little exploration, trial, and testing.

Cummins Nursery lists 197 heirloom apples on their site. And the English apple website Orange Pippin lists 761 varieties (not all heirloom) to explore: https://www.orangepippin.com.

Black Oxford—Photo Credit Cummins

Often, the human connection makes an heirloom variety of special value. I remember the late Michael Phillips, author of *The Apple Grower*, speaking highly of the Black Oxford apple variety. It just seems to ripen too late for my region, even though it is hardy enough to survive our winters.

4. Help Strengthen Local Food and Gardening Culture

Once you catch on to following the spindle method outside its usual commercial environment, you may feel moved to share both your knowledge and perhaps some of your homegrown trees with local schools, senior living communities, community gardens, food banks, and so on. Hearing and responding to the needs of fellow gardeners is so satisfying.

When I was a school garden teacher, I was fine having some October apples. That was perfect: we could pick and store them for fresh use, make muffin-sized pies, and share them with families, students, and shelters. Yet last year I met a schoolteacher who runs a summer garden program near a mobile home park for underserved children, and I realized I could graft July- and August-ripening apple varieties and donate them, so she had something to fresh developing for her students in those months.

I also imagine apple gardeners introducing specialty culinary varieties to local growers to market to local artisanal bakeries, including pay-what-you-can cafes that might want to cultivate a few small trees in their kitchen garden. As a garden educator with no current program of my own, cultivating community connections is my new field of dreams: promoting gardens that grow people.

CALL TO ACTION—Start planning your new apple garden today and visit my website at https://www.manzanitatlc.com/ so that together we can build a supportive community of apple gardeners who share solutions and challenges!

I'm also looking forward to getting this information into the hands of arborists and tree enthusiasts who understand "right tree, right place"—yet haven't yet seen the potential for spindle trees outside the usual commercial context. Fortunately, apple trees thrive in a wide variety of locations. It's just a matter of choosing the right variety and rootstock.

Trees in general, not just apples, are good in so many ways that we might think of encouraging tree planting to grow gardeners and community. We can promote living Christmas trees, Birthday Trees / Memorial Trees / School Trees / and even recognizing Champion or Historic Trees. Local Arborists and other plant Nerds can tell you more about Champion Trees and often maintain websites listing the biggest trees in your area.

www.ingramcontent.com/pod-product-compliance
Lightning Source LLC
Chambersburg PA
CBRC101827090426
42811CB00024B/1921